Quiche Isn't Sexy

A Play in One Act

By Gabriel Davis

gabriel@alumni.cmu.edu
gabrielbdavis.com

Cast

3 women, 3 men

Characters

Jay
Jackie
Moderator
Guy 1
Guy 2
Lady

SCENE 1: A meeting of Meat Eaters Anonymous.

> (The group sits in a circle or semi-circle with audience on the other side).

MODERATOR

Go on …

JAY

Hello, my name is Jay and I'm a burger addict.

GROUP

Hello, Jay.

JAY

Savory, juicy patties on fluffy white buns fill my heart. Probably with grease.

GUY 1

I been there.

GUY 2

Amen, brother.

JAY

My doc quit his practice to follow his Broadway dreams. He still sees a couple patients backstage during intermission.

LADY

Aw, that's nice.

JAY

But you have to pay for and sit through his shows.

GUY 1

I had a dentist like that.

JAY

He's currently in Cats.

                              GROUP
                (Collective groan and assorted comments like:)
Oh boy. Man. Ouch. I love Cats!

                               JAY
So, it's intermission of Cats. He takes my vitals and sing-diagnoses me.
"Well, Jay you've got …"
                    (singing, to tune of the Rolling Stones "Angie")
"Angi, angina, it's from the burgers I fear. With no spinach in your soul
and no quinoa in your bowl, you can't say you're satisfied?"

                             JACKIE
Wow, nice pipes, Jay.

                               JAY
Thanks!   So … his lyrics floor me. I run out and don't stay for the second
act.

                              LADY
Of Cats? That's the best part.

                              GUY 1
I didn't realize there was a second act.

                              GUY 2
Yeah, I just followed the mass exodus to the parking lot when I went.

                               JAY
Next thing I know I'm at a gastro pub slinging back Angus sliders, and the
barmaid is staring at me. "What?" I ask. "You might want to slow down
there" she says "you know every time a cow farts, it puts a hole in the
ozone." I laugh a little, her stare sharpens like a dagger. "I'm not joking
man" she says, "It takes hundreds of millions of cows to keep your Angus
sliders flowing. The ecological footprint they leave collectively is worse
than every automobile on the planet combined."

                              GUY 1
Didn't leave a tip, didja?

                              JAY

I complained to the manager …

                             GUY 1

Well done.

                              JAY

 … and they fired her.

                             GUY 2

Oooh.

                              JAY

As I watched her curse me and storm out, I got to thinking.   Is she right?
Are burgers hurting more people than just me?

                             LADY

At rock bottom, I once killed a man for a burger.

                             GUY 1

I used to dress up like the Hamburglar.

                              JAY

That's not so bad.

                             GUY 1

And burglarize fast food joints.   One time I broke into a 24-hour
McDonalds after they closed.

                             LADY

When would a 24-hour McDonalds close?

                             GUY 1

Right, but I was strung out on Shamrock Shakes at the time. Anyway,
some other guy dressed like Ronald McDonald caught me in the meat
locker shoving frozen patties into my costume.   That creepy clown kicked
the frozen patties out of me.

                              JAY

Oh … so … um anyway … that night, the waitress' words still echoed in my mind.

GUY 2
(Doing a lady's voice and echo effect on "me")
"Are burgers hurting more than just me, me, me, me, me, me"

JAY
Something like that. I look at the burger stack on my bedside table and begin to shed tears of guilt. I put a burger in my mouth and suck on it like a meat pacifier to calm myself down. And I drift to sleep. I dream I am living in ancient times, part of a lost burger-loving civilization. Hieroglyphics of burgers line the walls of our cave dwellings. The cows all have names like "Steero the Elder", "Vealo the Younger," "Goldie the Yummy." And it's Goldie's turn to be dinner.

LADY
I once purchased an entire cow named Ethel. It tastes better when you know the cow's name, don't you think?
(A few nods of agreement from the group)

JAY
So, in my dream, the tribesman want to have something special. I suggest adding bacon. They all get very excited and nominate me to prepare the sacred dinner. I set off to satisfy the cravings of my people. I ascend meaty mountain, where bacon bushes grow wild along flowing streams of mayonnaise. I gather these toppings and descend the mountain.

JACKIE
Like Moses?

GUY 1
Oh, I get it, he's like a bacon-loving Moses in his dream!

LADY
Wouldn't Moses have kept Kosher?

GUY 2
The subconscious wants what the subconscious wants.

MODERATOR

Let's let him finish.

JAY

On my way down the mountain, I can see the tribesman below dancing in a frenzied circle around Goldie. Two of the tribesman with larger bellies grab their chests and fall over. A loud crack of thunder can be heard. A puff of black gas emerges from Goldie's behind and rises up into the air merging with a monolithic black cloud that hovers above my people. The tribesman come into focus, I realize, they all look exactly like me. It's a whole tribe of me! I call down to my selves. "Look at you! Worshipping Goldie the Calf!" The bushel of bacon in my right arm grows heavy, the clay bowl of mayo balanced on my head begins to wobble. I allow both to fall. On the ground I see two stone tablets. I call out to my selves "You must cease your worship of Goldie the Calf! From this day forward you shall follow these tablets!" I pick them up and reveal on the first tablet - a chickpea! On the second - kale! My selves look up at me, Goldie makes a run for it, sun parts the clouds. I am exalted. The sun begins to pulsate and beep loudly. My alarm, waking me up. I open my eyes and remove the burger from my mouth.

MODERATOR

Awesome! Removing the burger from your mouth is the first step on the road to recovery!

JAY

Ever since, I've eaten beans and nuts and shit.

MODERATOR

Wonderful. Can we all encourage Jay?

GROUP

(Half-heartedly)
Yay. Go Jay. Great job. Way to show your bedside burgers who's boss.

JACKIE

So how's it going with all that kale and beans and nuts and stuff?

JAY

It sucks. Sometimes I try to shape them into patties. It's not the same. But my cholesterol is getting better and I don't cry when I eat them.

GUY 2

Keep on keeping on, brother.

JAY

So ... thanks for listening guys. In case you missed it before, my name is Jay...and I'm a recovering burger addict.

MODERATOR

Thank you, Jay. Welcome to Meat Eaters Anonymous. We're really glad to have you with us.
     (beat)
Alright folks, that does it for today's meeting. We'll see everyone next week.

     (People start clearing out. Jay and Jackie both get to water cooler at same time.)

JAY

After you.

JACKIE

Thanks.

     (Jackie pulls an obscenely large water bottle out of her bag and begins filling it. They stand there for a while as she fills the bottle. Jay shifts his weight getting a little impatient. A few people come up to Jay and welcome him to the group, improvise basic hellos here, welcome to our group, etc. and then exit. When everyone is gone, Jackie is STILL filling her water bottle. If required for the bit, have her pull multiple bottles out of her bag as each is filled OR escalate the size graduating to a half gallon container ... play with it. But throughout the entire exchange below she should be filling bottles).

JAY

Water shortage in your building?

JACKIE

I never drink tap. My body is my temple.
> (Beat)

Except when I gorge on mutton.

JAY

You're … a lamb addict?

JACKIE

Well, I said mutton. Mutton is an adult sheep. Lamb is a sheep less than a
year old.

JAY

Oh, ok.

JACKIE

I'm not a pervert. You think I'm into baby sheep or something?

JAY

Ah …

JACKIE

I'm just messing with you. I used to eat lamb, hogget, which is
adolescent sheep, and mutton. I didn't care. If it went "bah," I'd eat it.

JAY

Ok.

JACKIE

So … burger addict … was that restricted to just cow-based burgers?

JAY

I've had other types of burgers.

JACKIE

Mutton burgers?

JAY

I don't think I've had mutton burgers, per se.

                    JACKIE
          (Judgy)
Uh-huh.
          (Long Beat)
And now you eat chickpea-kale burgers?

                    JAY
I eat chickpea-kale sandwiches. The word "burger" is like a trigger for me.

                    JACKIE
Plus let's face it, they're nothing like burgers.

                    JAY
No.

                    JACKIE
So how many days sober?

                    JAY
So far … two months meat free.   You?

                    JACKIE
One year last week.

                    JAY
Wow.

                    JACKIE
Yeah.

                    JAY
What do you eat?

                    JACKIE
Well, I haven't sworn off eggs and cheese … so a lot of eggs and cheese.
And crackers.
          (beat)
So long as it's not meat, I can count myself sober.

                    JAY

My doctor did say I can have a few eggs once a week.

                              JACKIE
Oh yeah?

                              JAY
I found a Quiche recipe … looks kind of interesting.

                              JACKIE
Interesting.

                              JAY
You wouldn't want to … try it?

          (Blackout)

Scene 2: Jay's apartment.

          (At dinner table, he serves the Quiche)

                              JAY
And here you go!

                              JACKIE
          (Fake enthusiasm)
Wow!

                              JAY
Quiche!

                              JACKIE
Yep, Quiche..

                              JAY
Dig in!

                              JACKIE
Ok...
          (About to take a bite)

Yeah... So I probably should have said this before you made the Quiche. You consider this a date, right?

                    JAY
I ... I thought it was a... What did you think?

                    JACKIE
Well here's the thing... Quiche isn't Sexy. I think people who eat Quiche are pretentious.

                    JAY
Yeah ... it probably would have helped if you had mentioned that ... previously.

                    JACKIE
I'm not saying I don't appreciate you made it. I just think Quiche is pretentious. Quiche is just an egg trying to be more than breakfast.

                    JAY
But you do eat a lot of eggs, right?

                    JACKIE
That was a metaphor.

                    JAY
I mean ... you said you eat a lot of eggs and cheese and crackers.

                    JACKIE
I said it metaphorically.

                    JAY
It seems kind of like a literal statement.

                    JACKIE
It's sweet that you had me over, tried to prepare me dinner. But this is a pretense of dinner. Isn't it?

                    JAY
I feel like it's a real dinner. Made out of food.

JACKIE

This is basically an omelet disguising itself as a savory pie. It's the perky beginning to one's day when it should be the lusty end.   When you think eggs ... do you think romance?

JAY

Is there some other food that you'd ... prefer?

JACKIE

You could have made ... a rack of lamb ...

JAY

Well, no, you're a meat addict so that'd be ...

JACKIE

Rare and wonderful.

JAY

I was going to say "destructive."

JACKIE

At first we'd take our knives and cut off little pieces. Small bits of juicy meat combined with the perfect combination of spices, rosemary and salt and ... small bites would turn to large bites and soon we'd have the lamb bones in our hands and we'd be devouring them. After, we'd devour each other.
        (Beat)
Before you ask. No, I don't mean literally ... I mean metaphorically ... and also sexually.

JAY

What now?

JACKIE

You'd devour me sexually. I'd devour you sexually.

JAY

If I'd made lamb... you'd have ...

JACKIE

Devoured you ....

                    JAY
... sexually?

                    JACKIE
Yes, now that I'm saying it out loud, it does sound strange .. but it
wouldn't feel strange. I'd like to be devoured by a man who cooks
wonderful lamb.
        (Beat)
You look ... uncomfortable ... Delicious food should be devoured. Great
sex should be delicious and impossible not to devour ... you can't help
yourself. You feel ... almost starved as you first approach each other. You
try to start slow but a speed, a ... something drives you to go faster and
faster to ... rip the meat from the bones, and you don't care if you get
covered in juices and flesh because you're ... well, you're not eating a
Quiche. A Quiche is eaten in tiny, dainty bites. Do you want to take me in
tiny, dainty bites?

                    JAY
No.

                    JACKIE
Do you want me to take you in tiny dainty bites?

                    JAY
        (Thinking about that, maybe trying to visualize what it would be
        ...)
Well ...

                    JACKIE
One does not devour a Quiche. And by serving me a Quiche, you are
telling me something. And that's why, as sweet as this gesture is ... I have
to tell you. It's not romantic ... it's the pretense of romantic. It's two
children kissing on the lips and exchanging promise rings. You know ... an
egg is basically immature chicken. We haven't hatched, you see. We've
tried. We've gone through the motions. We've rubbed the sticks together
but there ... there is no fire. It really does look good on the plate though.
But let's face it. Neither you, nor I are interested in what you've put on
the menu. Ok then. Well ... Goodnight.

(She turns and heads toward the door)

                              JAY

Wait …
          (Beat)
You like things that go …

                              JACKIE

"Bah"

                              JAY

Do you like such things … ground up?

                              JACKIE

Like a burger?

                              JAY

What if I run down to the bodega and get some lamb and grind it up and
fry it up and put it on a bun and we eat it and then we …

                              JACKIE

Destroy ourselves.

                              JAY

Right, bad idea.

                              JACKIE

Yeah.
          (Points to herself)
One year sober.

                              JAY

Yep.

                              JACKIE

Well, goodnight.

                              JAY

Goodnight.

(They both stand there. She doesn't turn to go)

                              JACKIE

How far is that bodega?

                              JAY

Less than five minutes away.

        (Blackout)

        (Lights up, they're both stuffing large lamb burgers into their
        mouths, furiously devouring them like people who haven't eaten
        in weeks. Moans, grunts and other appropriate noises of
        pleasure. The whole segment is a flash, a few moments to get the
        feel of deep satisfaction they are experiencing. The actors
        needn't actually swallow the food even … it can be that they are
        just overfilling their mouths insanely and chewing and grunting
        joyfully and then …)

        (Blackout)

        (Lights up, they are both sitting at the table, sated and spent.
        Plates are empty)

                              JAY

So, should we have sex now?

                              JACKIE

I'm stuffed. The thought of …

        (He agrees)

                              JAY

Yeah.
        (Beat)
Plan B. Gallon of maple bacon ice cream while watching Netflix. Then
pass out.

                              JACKIE

Perfect.

(Blackout again)

Scene 3: A series of Meat Eater's Anonymous meetings.

(Lights up. Jay and Jackie are at the Meat Eaters Anonymous group again. Some weeks have passed. They have small pot-bellies now.)

GUY 1

…. and I'm just staring at my brother's plate, he's pouring beef gravy on this incredible hot roast beef sandwich he has, and I look down at my plate and … I've got this spinach salad and this raspberry vinaigrette to pour on mine…
(Breaking down, weeping)
I'm weak, I'm so weak.

MODERATOR

Temptations are everywhere. What's important is how we … resist.

GUY 1

I buried my face in his sandwich and just started chewing and sucking.

LADY

I've done that.

GUY 2

Been there, brother.

LADY

I was into meat masks for awhile. The beef gravy does wonders for the complexion.   Just let it dry on there. Then peel if off in strips like beef Jerky.

MODERATOR

Well … We all slip, we all slip. What's important is that we pick ourselves back up again.
(Beat)
Does anyone else have anything they'd like to share today?

(Beat)
Jackie and, um …

                    JAY
Jay.

                    MODERATOR
We haven't seen you two for a few weeks. Anything you'd like to share?

                    JACKIE
Nothing new. Just been busy.

                    JAY
Fightin' the good fight.

                    MODERATOR
Well, now is the time for resolve. With Thanksgiving just around the
corner we're all going to be tested.

          (Blackout. Lights back up a moment later. Both Jay and Jackie
          have bigger bellies now)

                    GUY 2
… and we sit down to Christmas dinner and everyone is eating juicy thick
slices of ham and I'm just eating … yam…

                    LADY
Pour some maple syrup on it. That helps.

                    MODERATOR
Well, you resisted, that's the important thing, Steve.   Let's all give Steve a
hand.
          (Everyone claps. Exclamations like "Great job Steve! Nice going
          Steve!" Etc.)
So … anyone else want to share anything? Any news?
          (Beat)
Everyone backslides and, you know it's nothing to be ashamed of. That's
what we're here for. Honesty and support. Honesty and support.
          (She's sort of focused on Jackie and Jay).

Jackie, Jay … you haven't shared for a few weeks. Anything you want to tell us?

                              JAY
Oh, no – no, all good here.   You know it's tough but … just gotta be strong. 4 months sober!

                            JACKIE
 Yep, one year two months for me!

          (Blackout. Lights back up, bellies on Jay and Jackie are even
          bigger)

                          MODERATOR
Wow, how time flies.   Can you believe spring is here already?
          (Beat)
So Jackie and Jay – anything you want to share?

                            JACKIE
Nope.   One year five months sober.

                              JAY
7 months sober!

          (Blackout. Lights up, bellies are huge and their faces and shirts
          are even covered in some meat juice).

                            GUY 1
Ok, this is getting ridiculous.

                          MODERATOR
Jackie, Jay. The, um, the group has voiced some concerns to me that perhaps you are not being totally open about your struggles. And we wanted you to know … we're here for you, if there's anything you want to say?

                            JACKIE
Just that I'm excited for Octoberfest!

                              JAY

Yeah, we know a lot of people here are struggling with all the bratwurst that's going to be at these things, but we just like the craft beers.

                    GUY 2
Is that meat juice on your faces?

                    JAY
Huh, what now?

                    LADY
I mean you expect us to believe you've each gained over a hundred pounds since last fall just eating kale?

                    MODERATOR
What Lisa is trying to say is …. We know that sometimes when couples who … when two people struggle with the same addiction, they can end up enabling each other.   It's easier to backslide …

                    GUY 1
Yeah, like backsliding right into the food & wine section of the New York Times.

                    LADY
Oh, I always throw that section right in the trash.

                    GUY 2
Yep, me too. Too tempting.

                    GUY 1
Well, I read it. It's my guilty pleasure.   It doesn't hurt to look.
          (Beat)
And to my surprise who do I see in this weekend's section but these two!
          (Pointing at Jackie and Jay. Pulls out the page of the newspaper
          he's talking about. Clears his throat)
"A new champion emerges amidst the city's finest meat-centric food trucks surpassing such formidable mobile masters of grease as Frittes and Meats and Steak-N-Take. Its name: Addictive Burger Blends.   And they are. With absolutely no background in food services, self-professed "meat addicts" Jackie Carter and Jay Gold, say an uncontrollable urge drove them to try over 2,000 different meat blends until they found the

one that they said will literally ruin your tongue for any other food and make your synapses explode with a dopaminergic rush that, incidentally, a team of scientists at Columbia are currently studying ... but that's a tale for another article. While the exact blend they use is proprietary and secret, they have revealed that it includes a mix of lamb, mutton, veal, chuck, sirloin, pork belly, and bacon dipped in goose fat and nestled within a light butter-toasted brioche that soaks in all the juices and dissolves in your mouth like divine meaty cotton candy. This reviewer will admit, and without shame, that when I took my first bite of this burger I literally shit my pants. I shit my pants and I didn't care. It was that good."

                                    LADY
You own a food truck!?

                                    GUY 2
Written up in the Times!

                                    JACKIE
It's a big city. Lot of people with the same names.

                                    GUY 1
                    (Turning page to face them)
Your pictures are in the article.
                    (Passes the picture around)

                                    JAY
With over 8 million people there are bound to be other people with the same names as us and similar faces. It's a numbers' game.

                                    MODERATOR
                    (Holding the paper)
You're saying this isn't you?

                                    JAY
Nope. Over a year sober.

                                    JACKIE
But I do happen to have their business cards and truck schedule handy.

(Starts passing them out. Some people throw them down, others
slip them into their pockets).

                    MODERATOR
Seriously?

                        JAY
Not for them, just if they have interested friends and family.

                       GUY 1
What you two are playing with, it's … Dante's descent into the inferno.

                     JACKIE
A flame-broiled, juicy, delicious inferno.
        (Beat)
I mean, ideologically I'm all for vegetarianism.

                        JAY
But if you have to eat meat …. If we were to be selling it.

                    MODERATOR
Pushing it.

                        JAY
We would use only Kobe-style cows, grass-fed and massaged blissfully all
their days.

                     JACKIE
Sheep and pigs that roam free of pens on small family farms.

                    MODERATOR
There's no such thing as humane meat.

                     JACKIE
But physically we crave it, don't we?

                    MODERATOR
Recent studies show red meat is probably definitely linked to cancer.

                     JACKIE

But it tastes so good.

She's a demon!

She's a witch! And he's a warlock!

JAY
We're just part of the fastest growing trend in America!

JACKIE
Take the Finch Public House in Atlanta. Each night, they prepare only 24 handcrafted hamburgers. At 10 p.m. a bell rings and someone shouts "Burger Time!" By 10:01pm all 24 burgers have been sold.

GUY 2
They're not … wrong. The gourmet burger industry generates hundreds of millions in revenue per annum.

JAY
People want burgers.

MODERATOR
No, they want to be healthy, happy – to leave an environmentally responsible ecological footprint. To treat their bodies and the planet right …
        (Beat, looking around at the group)
Right?

JAY
Anyway, we know where we're not wanted. You guys… stay strong!
        (Burger in wrapper falls out of his pocket)
Let's go Jackie.
        (They start to exit)

GUY 1
Did you seriously just drop a burger out of your pocket just now?

JAY

No. That? That's not mine.

                            JACKIE
Not ours. Bye guys.

        (Jay and Jackie exit. The group's eyes go to the burger on the
        floor. A tense moment. They lunge for it – all but the moderator
        – fighting over it like animals. Some manage to grab pieces of it
        and stuff the pieces hungrily into their mouths. Blackout).

                        END OF PLAY

Printed in Great Britain
by Amazon